ART DECO COSTUMES

BY GEORGE BARBIER

INTRODUCTION BY

MADELEINE GINSBURG

CURATOR FROM THE DEPARTMENT OF TEXTILE
FURNISHINGS AND DRESS
VICTORIA AND ALBERT MUSEUM
LONDON

BRACKEN BOOKS
LONDON

PUBLISHED BY BRACKEN BOOKS
AN IMPRINT OF BESTSELLER PUBLICATIONS LTD
PRINCESS HOUSE, 50 EASTCASTLE STREET
LONDON W1N 7AP
ENGLAND

ART DECO COSTUMES
REPRODUCES THE COMPLETE PLATES FROM THE ALMANACS
FALBALAS ET FANFRELUCHES
BY GEORGE BARBIER
MEYNIAL
PARIS
1922-1926

ACKNOWLEDGEMENTS
THE AUTHOR WOULD LIKE TO EXPRESS
GRATEFUL THANKS FOR THE ASSISTANCE OF
VICTOR ARWAS, CELESTINE DARS, ERTÉ,
PHILIPPE GARNER, SUE LAMBERT,
JACK PALMER WHITE, CHARLES SPENCER,
FRANÇOISE TÉTARD-VITTU, GILLIAN
VARLEY, LEO DE WAAL.

POSTER ART SERIES

ISBN 1 85170 155 9
PRINTED IN ITALY

INTRODUCTION

'George Barbier is one of the most precious and significant artists of our era . . . When our times are lost . . . in the dust . . . some of his watercolours and drawings will be all that is necessary to resurrect the taste and the spirit of the years in which we have lived'.

When Albert Flament wrote this tribute in 1922 Barbier was only forty. Acclaimed at his first exhibition in 1911, he swiftly reached the peak of his profession, a position he was to hold throughout his short lifetime. Imaginative, but not eccentric; colourful and never garish; detailed, but not pedantic; entirely French in its elegance and restraint, his work appealed to high and lowbrow alike. His range was wide and he illustrated books for all ages, designed costumes for film, theatre and ballet, as well as fashions for the couture and the ready-to-wear. A member of the *Société des Artistes Décorateurs*, he also designed jewellery, glass and wallpaper. He wrote well, and his essays, especially those in the *Gazette du Bon Ton* (between 1915 and 1925) and the prefaces to his books, put his illustrations into the context of his life and attitudes.

His work covers the period generally referred to as the Age of Art Deco, the term taken from the 1925 *Paris Exposition Internationale des Arts Décoratifs et Industriels Modernes*. Here were displayed the finest artifacts of the period in styles ranging from elegant neo-classicism, like that of Barbier, via *faux* naive folk art to the extremes of abstract and streamlined modernism. But by 1932, the year of Barbier's death, the plutocratic optimism of the social and artistic post-war world had disappeared, submerged in economic slump and decline.

In the years that followed Barbier's work was scattered, the fine prints and illustrated books (mainly limited editions) locked away as prized collectors' items, the fashion illustrations deprived of their contexts, and the film and theatre costumes became a fading memory. It is indeed fortunate that *Falbalas et Fanfreluches*, the original publication from which the plates in this book are taken, has survived as a whole and that it illustrates such a wide spectrum of his work. Reflecting his interests, professional and personal, it provides a picture of Paris, the fashionable as well as the social and artistic capital of the inter-war years. Published as a series of illustrated almanacs from 1922 to 1926, it succeeded a series in smaller format, *La Guirlande des Mois*, 1917–21, which Barbier had illustrated for the same publisher, Meynial and which was contemporary with their *Bonheur du Jour* or *Les Graces à la Mode*, 1920–24, a portfolio of very fine illustrations produced to mark the return of peace. The pictures in *Bonheur du Jour* were restricted to the contemporary social scene but in the introduction Barbier outlined his ambition to provide a *Trachtenbuch*, or costume picture book, of the type that had originated in the late sixteenth century; intended to appeal to lovers of the costume and dress of many lands and periods, it would also record contemporary fashions for posterity.

In *Falbalas et Fanfreluches* Barbier extends his coverage of the social scene and adds illustrations of folk, historic and theatrical costume. The format follows that of the almanac, first introduced in the early seventeenth century, and each of the five wove paper volumes (253 × 160 mm) contains a diary and note page, rather minimal *raison d'être*, and an introductory essay headed with a black line block vignette. Printed in photogravure and coloured in stencil and watercolour, the almanacs have decorative covers and contain twelve plates, one for each month. Each of these vignettes, headed with a rather haphazardly printed date and location, has a descriptive or allusive title, and the lively, colourful little figures outlined in black, neat and flat with minimal modelling, are set against a background almost like a theatre drop. Formal and decorative, they have something of the pictorial quality of the Japanese prints and Mogul miniatures which were the inspiration of Barbier and of his contemporaries. The essays, all on aspects of fashion, and each by one of his friends – ladies of the highest social and intellectual prestige – give the almanacs a further significant dimension.

The Comtesse de Noailles begins, writing Barbier a letter on contemporary styles and a woman's ability to convey and change mood by altering her appearance. One of the most significant French women poets and novelists of the first half of the century, she was a great literary hostess and friend of Proust and Cocteau as well as Barbier. Intriguingly, a photograph in *Les Modes*, 1922, shows her likeness to the ideal Barbier lady – tiny, fragile, with large dark eyes, rosebud lips and pointed chin. She also wears the Venetian *tricorne*, similar to several of Barbier's dramatic ladies in this first almanac, though the style was not uncommon.

Colette continues in 1923; in *Modes*, she comments on the contemporary taste for the reed slim, bob-haired beauty. One of the outstanding writers of modern times, just at the height of her career, she still had time to be interested in fashion, and indeed was about to open a beauty business on the Côte d'Azur!

Cecile Sorel, the actress, wrote the 1924 essay, *Coquetterie*, a subject which her famous role as Celimène, the teasing heroine of Molière's *Le Misanthrope*, had given her an almost vested interest. An inspired self publicist with great style and panache, she was equally well known for her off-stage as well as on-stage activities and credited, among other exploits, with a president of France dead in her bed and an ascent of the pyramids dressed *à la* Louis XIV. Within a few years she was to desert the legitimate stage for the music-hall, at the mature age of sixty.

Both Gérard d'Houville, otherwise Mme Henri de Règnier, and the Baronne de Brimmont, poets and novelists, continue the theme in 1925 and 1926 deploring the boyish austerity of the 1920s modes. Thus a total of five writers penned the same message – witty laments on the retreat of femininity before the new ideal, the *garçonne*, the boyish girl, a feeling which Barbier also shared. On the drawing board he idealizes them, enhancing their appearance with a variety of charming and inventive clothes. In his essay *Atalante* (*Gazette du Bon Ton*, 1924) he is more critical, deploring their bisexual appearance, asexual approach, ungraceful athleticism and inability to grow old gracefully. It was probably through his preference, as well as tribute to his prestige, that by the 1920s the fashion plates Barbier drew for *Bon Ton* were almost exclusively for Worth, the most senior and prestigious of the Paris couture houses, though artistically perhaps a little past its prime, making conservative, luxurious clothes for a mature clientele.

The drawings in the Worth Guard Books of designs were, like the Barbier vignettes, prepared six to twelve months ahead of the published mode. They make one of the most complete couture series of the period and are now in the Victoria and Albert Museum where they provide a useful group for comparison with the fashions in *Falbalas et Fanfreluches*. In 1921 the dresses were comparatively short, four inches below the knee for day though almost ankle length for evening. The waistline was at natural level but looked higher because of the tight bodice. The following year the longer bodice loosened and the hem, which was often arranged as an asymmetrical drape with a serpentine train, dropped. Flowing sleeves were a new feature. The trend continued through 1923, although hems had begun to rise for evening and many were fur trimmed. But in late 1924 styles began to change and dresses were made tighter and less draped, culminating in late 1925 in short hemlines just below the knee for day and only slightly longer for evening. Pleats provided room to move and sleeves, which had become tighter, began to flare at the wrist.

Although in general Barbier followed Worth trends there were significant differences, such as his preference for splashes of colour and bright peasant-style embroidery, a Poiret speciality; Chinese-style embroideries so popular with Callot Soeurs; and above all the *robes de style*, romantic recollections of mid-nineteenth-century styles, the speciality of Jeanne Lanvin. Finally, the dramatic rise in hem level in late 1925 is not recorded in Barbier's 1926 series. Perhaps this was an accident of chronology or else, like many of the general public, he preferred the skirt at mid-calf level. Accessories, though chic, are conventional and an unusual feature is the attention devoted to the shoes, details small enough to have been conventionalized by a less conscientious illustrator. But Barbier liked shoes: in *Les Pieds Nus* (*Bon Ton*, 1915) he expounds their charm and history. Unusually varied, they were always suited to the outfits they accompanied.

At least equal attention is given to the clothes worn by the men. After all, tall, good looking, with regular features and a small moustache, Barbier himself was notably elegant and fastidious. It is intriguing that so many of the star-crossed lovers in the narrative vignettes not only resemble one another but are fair haired as he himself was. As for his own clothes, he set out his preferences in *Smart* (*Bon Ton*, 1924): an understated elegance, in the *style anglaise*, without eccentricity or even undue individuality. No bright waistcoats, gaudy ties, socks or shoes but some of scarlet patent leather he does find rather tempting . . . The men in the illustrations are perhaps a little more *outré* than his ideal, but still aware of sartorial conventions, rigidly observed in France. For less formal occasions a dark jacket with grey flannel trousers was permissible and for the country or travelling a loose-fitting, belted Norfolk-jacket-type suit. An informal dinner party required a dinner suit, and formal occasions tails and a white tie. The suits he shows were in the height of French fashion with narrow shoulders, high button fastening, a short waist and a rounded body line. The medium-wide trousers had deep turn-ups and were above ankle length. They do not change although by the end of the period styles were beginning to alter, jackets to become more loosely cut with wider, square shoulders, and trousers wider and longer. Again the shoes were a feature, on the whole much more brightly coloured and higher heeled than was the elegant norm.

In the regional and historical scenes more attention was devoted to the clothes of the men than the ladies. Not only was Barbier interested in fancy dress, his illustration and stage work had given him great knowledge of the sources.

George Barbier was born in Nantes on 10 October 1882, and the influence of this busy seaport never left him. Its fine seventeenth- and eighteenth-century buildings, bustling, colourful trade with the East in ivory, lacquer and exotic fabrics, were a constant inspiration. He came from a solid middle-class background and trained first with two local artists only slightly older than himself, P. A. Lesage and A. Broca. On moving to Paris he studied at the *École des Beaux Arts* in the atelier of Jean-Paul Laurens who was known for his historical narrative paintings, precisely researched, dramatic, patriotic and cold in colour. They are said to have had little appeal for Barbier but their influence should not be discounted for it was probably here that he began to strengthen and broaden his interest in the past, the source for much of his success. Some of his story-book illustrations suggest that he absorbed the essentials of Laurens' style, but transmuted them for a more sophisticated twentieth-century clientele by miniaturizing, altering the colours, and above all adding the ultimate saving grace of humour.

Barbier himself suggested that the ultimate source of his inspiration was Greek and Etruscan art, especially the Tomb of the Dancers in Tarquinia which he found an artistic revelation. His assiduous study of classical sources confirmed his attitude to the human form. Unlike his modernist or abstract contemporaries he remained, as J. L. Vaudoyer noted in 1929, 'an idealist of the human form', the essential qualities of his art 'classical, traditional and bookish'. Statuesque, powerful yet graceful figures, formal in drawing yet anatomically correct, moving in profile against an economically detailed creamy-gold background, were to provide models and inspiration for the rest of his creative life, predictably perhaps for his illustrations from the classics but just as effective when enhancing luxurious couture dresses in the fashion journals.

Reserved, cool, Barbier considered himself an anglophile and during these early years adopted the Anglo-Saxon pseudonym E-W (Edward-William) Larry, the signature on some of his earliest work. These qualities ensured the success of his first exhibition in 1911 in rue Tronchet, for which the well-known classico-romantic novelist Pierre Loüys wrote an appreciative introduction.

Equally important was the influence of his fellow students at the *École des Beaux Arts*, especially the six hard-working, talented exquisites Bernard Boutet de Monvel, his cousin Pierre Brissaud, Jean Besnard, Paul Iribe, Georges Lepape and Charles Martin, all of whom rose to the heights of their profession. In 1922 *Vogue*, for whom they and Barbier had all worked, dubbed them 'The Knights of the Bracelet'. They were described as characterized by 'a certain dandyism of dress and manner . . . their hat brims are a wee bit broader than the modish . . . and worn with a slight tilt . . . to give the impression of fastidiousness. Their coats are pinched in just a little at the waist, and their boots are immaculate. A bracelet slipping down over the wrist . . . betrays a love of luxury'. The resemblance to the dapper little figures in *Falbalas et Fanfreluches* is inescapable. Barbier, unlike some of his fellow artists, was equally fastidious about his studio and worked surrounded by a fine collection of historical and exotic objects. Though reserved, he was said to be a charming companion and he became an habitué of Parisian literary high society

All the Knights of the Bracelet were, to a greater or lesser extent, affected by the same artistic trends, the turn-of-the-century style termed *Art Nouveau* which had culminated in the 1900 Paris *Exposition des Arts Décoratifs* and the subsequent reaction to it. Barbier retained to an unusual degree an affection for the art of the later eighteenth century which had, and indeed still has, a continuous appeal for the general public. Most noticeable in the graphic arts field was the effect of the Japanese prints and Persian and Mogul miniatures which shared the elevated viewpoint, the absence of middle ground, and flat but precisely detailed backgrounds, but added a rounded sensuality to the figures and additional richness of colour to the bright clear tones of the Japanese. The paintings of Matisse and the Fauves at the *Salons des Indépendants*, and their use of colour were a revelation to young painters. Everywhere muted pastels were in flight before this 'vivid sunburst of colour'. Barbier's own colour sense was widely admired: to Francis de Miomandre in 1914 it was 'a flourish of smiling colours' and, even more poetically to Henri de Règnier he was in 1929 producing 'the colour of life and the colours of dreams'. Poiret claimed credit for introducing the new palette to the world of fashion and interior design but its general acceptance was confirmed by the tremendous reception of the rich and exotic sets and costumes of the Diaghilev ballet which arrived in Paris in 1909. Appreciation was not confined to the sets: balletomania was rife, Barbier among its happy victims. His drawings of Nijinski (1913) and Karsavina (1914) were among his earliest most popular works, and Pavlova became model, subject and friend. In later years he himself designed for the ballet so it is no accident that the little figures in *Falbalas et Fanfreluches* play out their scenes in ballet-like mime.

Also relevant were the family connections of this student group: Barbier's next, very successful exhibition, was at the Galerie Boutet de Monvel. He showed 92 works divided into groups which were to characterize his future output – *Danseuses*, in classical pose; *Ballets Russes*; *Belles du Moment*, fashionable and contemporary.

A chance meeting between magazine publisher Lucien Vogel and a mutual friend involved all six artists in a new luxury publication, the *Gazette du Bon Ton*, which was to confirm for all time the entry of art into fashion illustration, replacing precise representation with evocations of fashionable mood and atmosphere. The ground had been laid by Poiret who had involved Iribe and Lepape in illustrating his 1908 and 1911 collections. Paquin followed in 1911, commissioning from them and Barbier

Eventails and *Fourrures*. In addition, together with Erté, a younger new recruit who was to become one of Barbier's close friends, they all designed clothes for the couture. Other, almost equally elegant magazines followed, such as the *Journal des Dames et des Modes* and *Modes et Manières d'Aujourdhui* and after the war *Art Goût Beauté* and the less specialized *Feuillets d'Art*, Barbier contributing to them all. However, the *Gazette du Bon Ton*, lasted longest, from 1911 to 1925 with a break during the war. It was a journal for the opulent hedonist – hand coloured, the sheets loose, thick and deckle edged – and the articles, many of which were contributed by Barbier, illuminated rather than illustrated. Barbier's early plates were somewhat Japanese in style, the figures asymmetrically placed with formal floral frames, but by 1915 the classical element, always strong, began to dominate. His illustration of the French couture contribution to the Panama Exhibition in 1915 has the figures linked in an almost Etruscan frieze against a pale gold sky.

For less esoteric journals such as *Vogue*, *Femina*, *Harpers* and *La Vie Parisienne* he worked in black and white, a medium in which he was as skilled as in gouache and watercolour.

Barbier's work continued throughout the war. His designs for Edmond Rostand's play *Casanova*, were very successful and were used for its three productions in Paris in 1918, then in New York and London, for the book and then for the film. Other theatrical work followed: *Lysistrata* (Maurice Donnay), *La Dernière Nuit de Don Juan* (Edmond Rostand), *Manon, Fille Gallante* (H. Bataille and A. Flament). Barbier had always loved the eighteenth-century style as many of the illustrations in *Falbalas et Fanfreluches* show, and no doubt enjoyed using his knowledge and experience for the costumes of the film *Monsieur Beaucaire*, an opulent and very expensive costume romp featuring Rudolph Valentino with art direction by his wife Natalia Rambova. Whatever their feelings about the film, the critics had nothing but praise for the clothes: 'gorgeous . . . never before have such wondrous settings and costumes been seen' enthused the *New York Times* at the opening in 1924. It is sad that photographs suggest that transatlantic 1920s taste triumphed over Barbier's historical accuracy. However, he was not deterred and in 1927 was designing sixteenth-century costumes for Dupuy Muznel's film, *Tournoi dans le Cité*.

Also during this period Barbier, like Erté, began to design for the *Folies Bergère*. The introduction that he wrote for Erté's 1929 exhibition evokes the atmosphere conjured by their designs: 'the magic carpet to a world of splendour . . . the large golden staircase . . . beautiful snowy women, their bodies almost immaterial . . . towering crowns and headdresses . . . sinuous robes resembling dragons held in leash'. Sadly, the small format of the almanacs can provide no more than a keyhole glimpse of such splendours.

In addition to all this activity, Barbier's illustrative work continued, commissions multiplying yearly. Some of his books were included in the very successful Book Design section of the 1925 Art Deco exhibition. His individual contribution was not noted in the jury reports but had already been marked by J. L. Vaudoyer in the 1924 *Studio Special Number on French Illustrated Books*. In addition to his artistic skill Barbier was unusually perceptive in his appreciation of the author's intentions, and it is no accident that so many of his 'clients', also became friends and eulogists. His colour sense, detail and delightful sense of humour made his work as appealing to children as to adults. With the stories he illustrated for Christmas numbers of *L'Illustration* between 1920 and 1929 he moves firmly into mainstream taste. No doubt the wide readership of this popular French family journal appreciated not only the colourful charm of his pictures but also what Francis de Miomandre, as early as 1914, had recognized as his freedom from 'isms' – the sole exception that universal panacea, escapism.

These pictures are the last strand in the inspiration which lies behind *Falbalas et Fanfreluches* for in 1932, at the height of his powers, he died. We can only endorse

Erté's epitaph: 'far too young'.

In 1929, Robert de Beauplan, writing in *L'Illustration*, considered Barbier 'one of the most characteristic witnesses of an age'. He underestimates, for the charm of his work transcends the merely modish to appeal across the decades to our own.

MADELEINE GINSBURG
CURATOR FROM THE DEPARTMENT
OF TEXTILE FURNISHINGS AND DRESS
VICTORIA AND ALBERT MUSEUM
MAY 1988

PLATE 1

The cover of the Falbalas et Fanfreluches
almanac of 1922.

Le Jeu des Graces.

Le Cadran Solaire.

PLATE 2

Left: Le cadran solaire (The sundial) *is shadowless under a sunfree sky, unable to mark the timeless (or temporary) grief of the fashionable couple. Even nature is sympathetic, the autumnal foliage reflecting their melancholy mood. She is very fashionable: her crossover bodice is tucked to cling to her slender boyish figure and the barrel-shaped skirt is softly pleated to the slightly low waistline. With it she wears a dramatic Venetian-type* tricorne *hat, which incidentally gives her an uncanny resemblance to the Comtesse de Noailles in the 1922* Les Modes, *and neat little buckled shoes. Her departing lover is dressed informally for the country in a loose suit, high waisted, its fullness retained with a half belt, cuff and pocket detail, and wide trousers.*

France XXᵉ siècle; *s & d George Barbier 1921; 1922 almanac.*

Right: Le jeu des Graces (The Graces at play) *gracefully in a formal garden, despite the very high heels of their unsuitable smart shoes. Their dresses look back to the immediate post-war period and have short sleeves, a wartime innovation, and midcalf-length full skirts which assist their easy movements. Their dresses still have high waistlines but the wide low belts point the way fashion is to go in the next few years. The girls left and centre have bobbed their hair, an innovation much criticized when introduced in 1915 during the war, but their playmate keeps her long hair arranged in a 'doorknocker' bun.*

France XXᵉ siècle; *s & d G. Barbier 1921; 1922 almanac.*

Le Jour & la Nuit.

Oui!

PLATE 3

Left: Oui! *The young lovers, their blissful accord symbolized by the pair of doves. Fugitives from a formal function, she wears a* robe de style *with a long fitted bodice, the low waistline marked by a flowing sash, the skirt composed of layers of cross-cut petal shapes. The style closely resembles a dress by the great French couturier Madeleine Vionnet, of the same date and colour, now in the Victoria and Albert Museum. He wears full evening dress with white tie and swallow-tailed coat with silk lapels, patent evening pumps and an unusual detail – white socks!*

France XXᵉ siècle; *s & d George Barbier 1921; 1922 almanac.*

Right: Le jour et la nuit (Day and night). *Posed in front of a scarlet rococo screen, the two guests at a fashionable fancy dress party confront one another. Day, arms akimbo, in her décolleté* robe de style, *oversized Spanish comb in her sleek black hair, confronts a speeding Night in dark lace-trimmed cloak over a Chinoiserie patterned skirt. Her fashionable head-dress, a beaded Phrygian cap, is softened with trailing osprey plumes.*

France XXᵉ siècle; *s & d George Barbier; 1922 almanac.*

La Toilette Délicieuse.

Papillons.

PLATE 4

Left: Papillons (Butterflies). *A summer idyll, even for the butterflies, which the lady launched in a leap inspired by the ballet arabesques Barbier loved to draw, is almost bound to miss. Her romantic pretty dress still retains the slight fullness above the waist typical of 1921, but the full sleeves are a 1922 feature. Note the back view of the popular* tricorne *hat worn by the lady in the foreground. Too exhausted to participate, the young man wears a light summer outfit with open-necked shirt and light trousers.*

France XXe siècle; *s & d George Barbier 1921; 1922 almanac.*

Right: La toilette délicieuse (The delightful dress) *being viewed in a fashion house which in its neo-classical detail resembles that of Poiret. The client wears the type of dress for which the house was known, simple with emphatic contrast trimming. The model shows an exotic evening dress with low-cut spangled bodice and panier drapes so fashionable in the early 1920s. The vendeuse, however, wears conservative, almost old-fashioned clothes, with a high waistline, high collar and neat midcalf-length boots with contrast toe and heel – easier on the feet of a working girl!*

France XXe siècle; *s & d George Barbier 1921; 1922 almanac.*

Elle et Lui.

PLATE 5

Elle et lui (She and he) *on a visit to Venice. In response to its notorious atmosphere of mystery and intrigue she conceals her eyes with a delicate veil suspended from her eighteenth-century-style* tricorne, *and is about to envelop her brown dress, with its fashionable long waist and gently full skirt, in a matching long caped, fur-lined and trimmed mantle. A flowing sash emphasizes the transition from high to low waistline which was to be achieved by 1922. Her companion is dressed for travelling in (probably English) tweeds and a Homburg hat. He wears spats, their cleanliness a reproach to the notorious Venetian puddles. In the sunset the white-clad gondolier grins knowingly, accustomed to Venice's reputation for assignations. Barbier's attitude to Venice was ambivalent: he loved its beauty and mystery and hated its decay.*

France XXe siècle; *s & d George Barbier 1921; 1922 almanac.*

L'Agression.

PLATE 6

L'Agression. *A sentimental interlude be-*
tween an Empire lady reclining on her
classical couch and a gallant Hussar dressed
to terrify – or to charm – the enemy in a
splendid uniform replete with braid and fur
trimming, sabre and sabretache by his side.
But the lady's little dogs, neither scared nor
charmed, defend their mistress and behind,
the statue of Eros the god of love unstrings
his bow. Barbier was knowledgeable and
fond of the early nineteenth-century prints
by Vernet and Debucourt, the probable
inspiration for this scene.

France XIXe siècle; *s & d George*
Barbier 1921; 1922 almanac.

Le Coq du Village.

L'Oiseau Cheri.

PLATE 7

Left: L'oiseau chéri (The darling bird). *The girl seems to have come from Wenthal, near Zurich, her dress typical with its cap with drooping frill, a floral chemisette and a jacket with contrast bound sleeves. But her young man, from his melon-topped pleated breeches supported by braces and red jacket, could have come from as far away as St Gall or Appenzell.*

Suisse XVIIIᵉ siècle; *s & d George Barbier 1921; 1922 almanac.*

Right: Le coq du village (The cock of the village). *The 1919 peace treaties increased awareness of eastern Europe, their colourful costumes becoming a lively new influence on fashion. These originated in Durnkolz, in the new European state of Czechoslovakia. The man is especially picturesque in his feather-trimmed hat, wide-sleeved shirt, braided breeches and tassel-trimmed boots. Though the girl has lost some of the traditional ribbon trimmings she has gained a floral apron.*

Tchéco Slovaque XIXᵉ siècle; *s & d George Barbier 1921; 1922 almanac.*

Le Langage des Fleurs.

Gentils propos.

PLATE 8

Left: Gentils propos (Sweet nothings). *An uncertainty about the new post-war boundaries has led Barbier to relocate the young couple who, from the dress of the man with his turned up hat, braid-trimmed trousers and full-sleeved shirt, probably came from Hungary.*

Tchéco Slovaque XIXᵉ siècle; *s & d George Barbier 1921; 1922 almanac.*

Right: Le langage des fleurs (The language of flowers). *From their clothes it would seem that this is another picturesque couple whom Barbier has mistakenly relocated! The young man wears a typical Hungarian shirt with wide sleeves, turned up hat and braid-trimmed breeches. The embroidered slipper socks illustrate the attention to detail.*

Tchéco Slovaque XIXᵉ siècle; *s & d George Barbier 1921; 1922 almanac.*

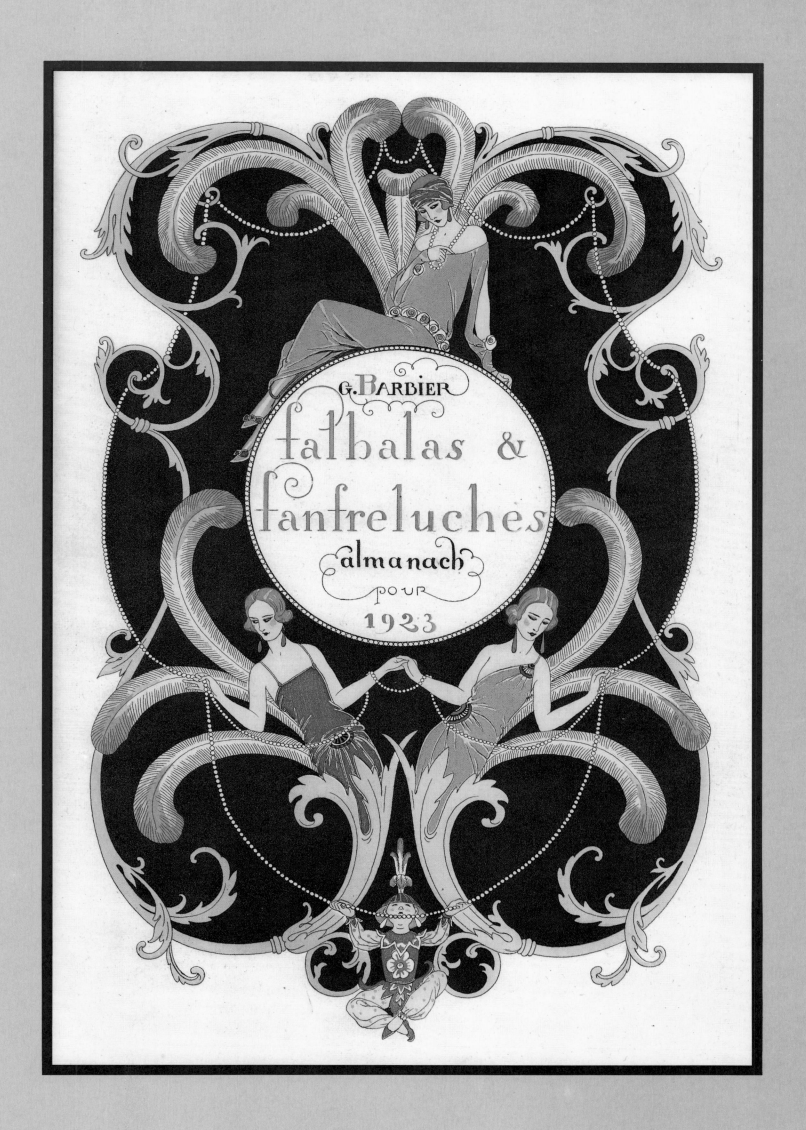

PLATE 9

The cover of the Falbalas et Fanfreluches *almanac of 1923.*

Le goul des chales.

La Villa d'Este

PLATE 10

Left: La Villa d'Este, *near Florence and on the terrace a lady in a formal afternoon dress with matching cloak and* tricorne *hat trimmed with fashionable large oriental-type motifs. She greets a young man in a light-weight summer travelling suit, loose, with high waistline and full-cut, above-ankle-length trousers. The deep pockets with buttoned flaps were a feature derived from First World War military uniforms. His accessories are interesting, a striped shirt with white cuffs and very high-heeled tan shoes.*

Tivoli Printemps 22. France XXe siècle; *s & d George Barbier 1922; 1923 almanac.*

Right: Le goût des châles (The fashion for shawls). *The ladies on the warm Mediterranian terrace wear bright coloured, large-pattern silk shawls, which it was fashionable to drape as dresses. Many were described as Spanish though actually embroidered in China, but others were from the fashionable French textile houses – indeed Barbier himself may have designed some of their fabrics. The large softly drooping feather fan was a fashionable accessory of the 1920s. The young man wears a dinner suit or Tuxedo, technically a full dress lounge suit, and black tie. He has an unusually ostentatious central stud on his starched shirt, a reminder of Barbier's exquisite youthful taste in jewellery.*

Capri Automne 22. XXe siècle; *s & d George Barbier 1922; 1923 almanac.*

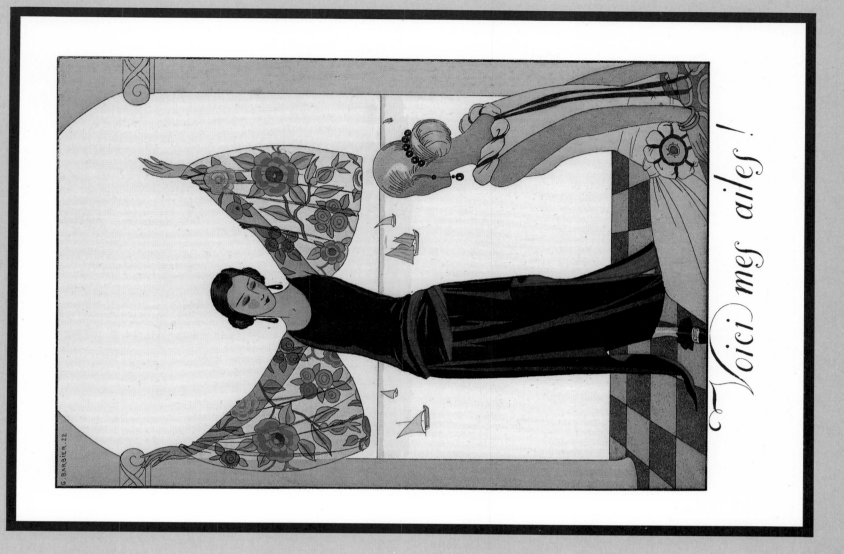

Voici mes ailes !

Incantation

PLATE 11

Left: Incantation (Solemn melody). *The pianist has a softly draped tunic with bold oriental pattern and fur-edged train, a feature of a Patou model in 1921. Her listener wears full evening dress, with oriental-style hip panels. The jewelled headband and crossed shoulder straps are similar to a formal outfit* (toilette de grand apparat) *worn by the Queen of Rumania and like the other dress, featured in* Les Modes *for 1921.*

France XXᵉ siècle; *s & d George Barbier 1922; 1923 almanac.*

Right: Voici mes ailes! (Look at my wings!), *and the lady shows off her new fashionable wide sleeves, spectacularly enhanced with brilliant coloured flowers. Her loose* robe d'intérieure (informal gown) *has a complex skirt, the red facing emphasizing the low waistline and the asymmetric trailing drapes at the hem. The lady seated in the foreground, in the more conventional evening dress, provides an excellent view of one of the longer hair styles fashionable at the beginning of the decade, the large low bun embellished with a decorative comb.*

France XXᵉ siècle; *s & d George Barbier 1922; 1923 almanac.*

Romance sans paroles.

PLATE 12

Romance sans paroles (Song without words). *An encounter between a sailor and a lady on the beach south of Naples in 1922. She wears a comparatively simple summer overdress with fashionable floating sleeves and low waistline with fullness from the hips. Her Japanese parasol is unusually plain.*

Sorrente Automne 22. France XXᵉ siècle; *s & d George Barbier 1922; 1923 almanac.*

La belle indolente

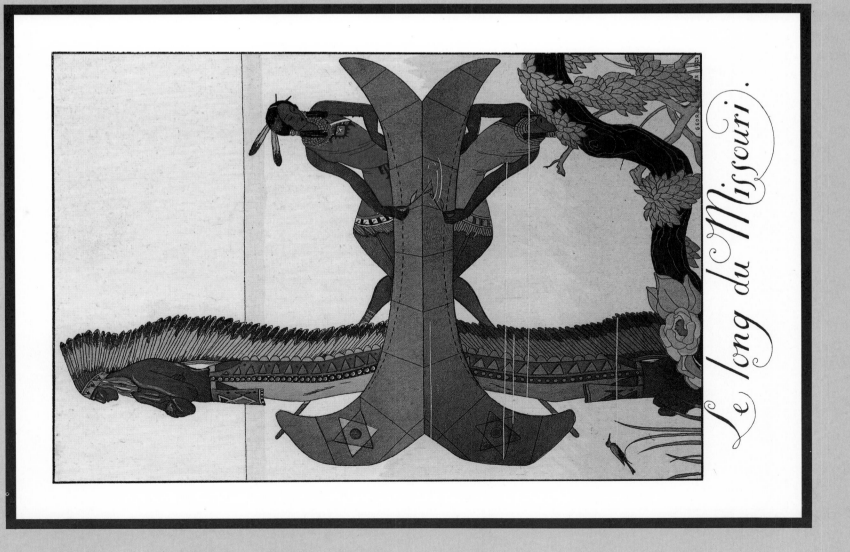

Le long du Missouri.

PLATE 13

Left: Le long du Missouri (Along the Missouri). *The red Indian was a picturesque figure well known to early cinema audiences. The pictorial treatment is ingenious, with the reflected image in the still water emphasized by the lower floral border.*

Amérique XIX siècle; *s & d George Barbier 1922; 1923 almanac.*

Right: La belle indolente (The lovely lazybones) *is an escapist evocation of French colonial life in the West Indies. The crinoline-clad Creole lady sways in her hammock, no doubt sipping a rum punch, while the market vendor in blouse, skirt and typical bandanna head-dress sells her water melons.*

Antilles XIX siècle; *s George Barbier; 1923 almanac.*

Venez donc, ma bonne amie!

N'ayez pas peur, petite!

PLATE 14

Left: N'ayez pas peur, petite! (Do not be afraid, little one!) *A scene perhaps inspired by the internationally famous and romantic adventures of Bonnie Prince Charlie who in 1745 escaped after his defeat in the Highlands, as much by charm as by judgement. Traditionally, the plaid mantle was worn by both men and women in the Highlands.*

Ecosse XVIII siècle; *s & d George Barbier 1922; 1923 almanac.*

Right: Venez donc, ma bonne amie! (Come along, dear!) *In 1816 Carl Vernet commemorated the Peace of Paris with a series of prints illustrating the mutual curiosity of the French and the English, so long kept apart by the wars of Napoleon. This is Barbier's version. The lady seems to be inquisitive about the Highlander's kilt . . .*

Ecosse XIXe siècle; *s & d George Barbier 1922; 1923 almanac.*

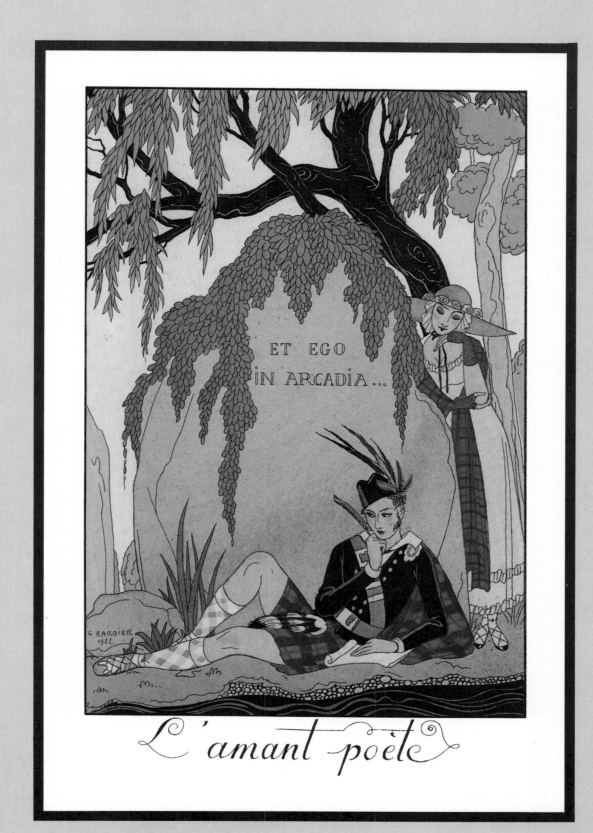

ET EGO
iN ARCADIA...

L'amant poète

PLATE 15

L'amant poète (The poetic lover). *A Scottish poet, in romantic pose, composes an ode to the vaguely Regency-style girl half hidden behind the rock on which he has begun his idyll with 'And I in Arcadia'. He wears full Highland dress with plume-trimmed Glengarry bonnet, kilt, sporran, tartan socks and lace-up brogues. The Highlands had been considered romantic ever since the days of poet and novelist Sir Walter Scott.*

Ecosse XIXᵉ siècle; *s & d George Barbier 1922; 1923 almanac.*

Entre deux feux.

La flûte de Pan.

PLATE 16

Left: La flute de Pan (Pan pipes). *Pausing amid the harvest are a couple from mainland Greece. The woman wears the type of dress associated with Athens, with semi-fitted sleeveless jacket over her embroidered shirt, and a belt with a large decorative buckle. The young man wears a cap with a tassel, short jacket, wide pleated skirt, the fustanella, and leggings. Popularised by the ephzones, the most picturesque regiment of the old Greek army, this outfit tended to be regarded as Greek national dress.*

Grèce XIX siècle; *s & d George Barbier; 1923 almanac.*

Right: Entre deux feux (Between two fires). *A designer's enthusiasm for the costume of eastern Europe is unaffected by political events. Here a Czech girl chooses between two young Hungarians with their wide-sleeved shirts and loose linen breeches.*

Tchéco Slovaque XXᵉ siècle; *s & d George Barbier 1922; 1923 almanac.*

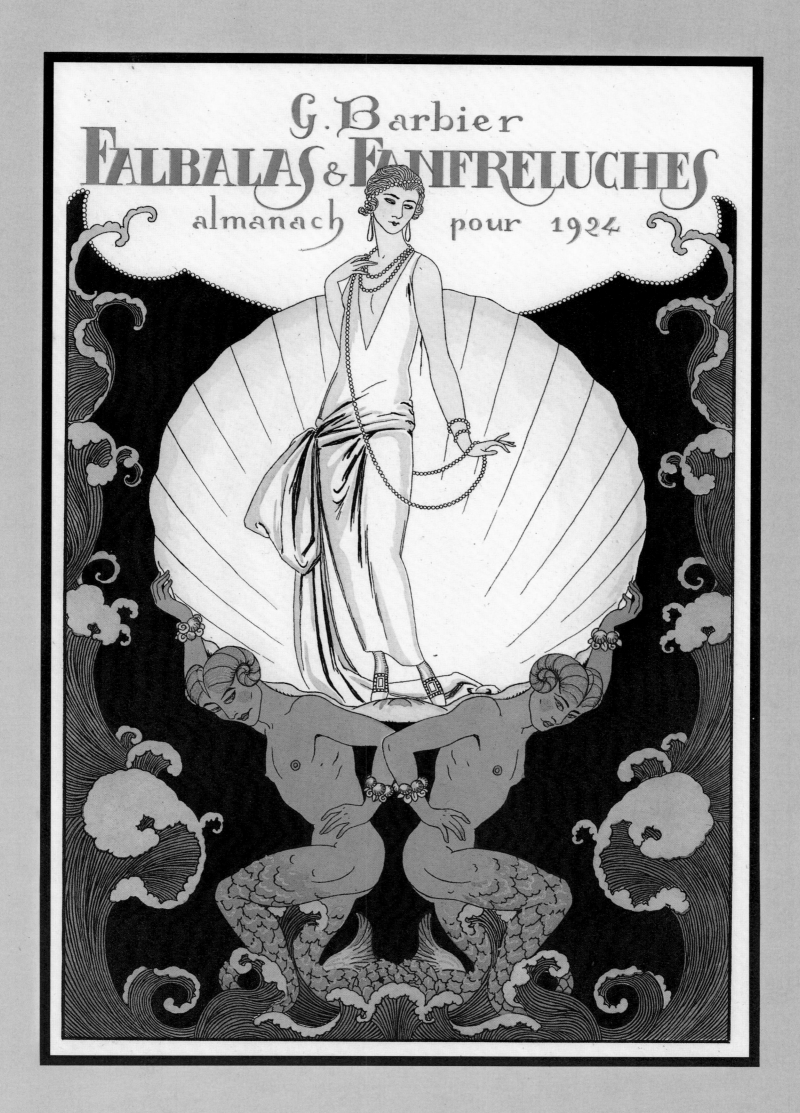

Mlle Sorel au bal du grand prix

Le Retour

PLATE 18

Left: Le retour (The return) *of a proud Gallic warrior in his traditional dress of winged helmet and cross-gartered breeches, to the embraces of his somewhat Hellenic looking wife, dressed anachronistically, so it would seem, by Poiret who featured several similar classical models in his earlier collections. In the corner of the picture the campaign, or at least the pursuit, continues.*

Epoque Gallo-Romaine; *s & d GB 1923; 1924 almanac.*

Right: Mlle Sorel au bal du grand prix (Mademoiselle Sorel at the bal du grand prix). *For the tableau at the grand annual Paris race ball she descends the stairs clad in fantastic Burmese guise, with towering pagoda-inspired cap and side hoops topped with feather palm fronds. Fantastic costumes of this type were made by many designers including Barbier and Erté. Cecile Sorel was at least fifty at the time of this sketch but her glamour transcended her years for Barbier and her many other fans.*

France XXe siècle; *s & d G. Barbier 1923; 1924 almanac.*

L'Escarpolette

PLATE 19

L'escarpolette (The swing) *and on it a
lady in a slim fitting summer dress, low-
necked and sleeveless, patterned boldly with
the art deco roses for which both Iribe and
Poiret claimed credit, a design introduced
in the years before the First World War.
The tones of the flowers on her bold striped
cloche hat are echoed by those of the scarf.
The black wristband into which her hand-
kerchief is tucked was a popular 1920s
accessory. The young man wears summer
clothes, a shirt and trousers.*

France XXe siècle; *G. Barbier 1923;
1924 almanac.*

L'Aveu difficile

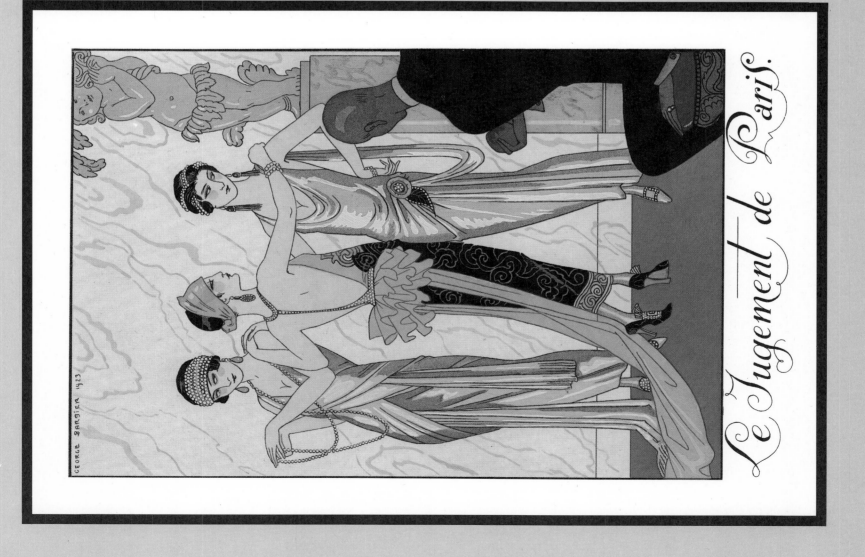

Le Jugement de Paris.

PLATE 20

Left: Le jugement de Paris (The judgement of Paris). *The ladies grouped in elegant competition could have purchased their dresses from several fashionable couturiers: Callot featured a dress with scarf drapes in 1923 and Worth the cross-draped fullness of the dress on the left in his collection of the same year. The central dress with colourful Chinoiserie embroidery may have been by Poiret who featured bustle-trimmed trains in 1924.*

France XXe siècle; *s & d George Barbier 1923; 1924 almanac.*

Right: L'aveu difficile (The difficult confession) *is made to a lady wearing a dress in extreme exotic taste, almost ancient Egyptian in inspiration, with the skirt tightly draped up to a central palmette and supported by a transparent yoke. The seated lady seems to have her dress held up by nothing at all – and completely strapless gowns were exceptional in the 1920s. It seems to be a wrap-around sarong-like drape, knotted at the hip and extending into a fashionable serpentine train. Is the pattern on the fabric the apple of temptation – or discord – or merely one of the many large-scale bright naturalistic patterns then fashionable?*

France XXe siècle; *s & d George Barbier 1923; 1924 almanac.*

La Jolie Insulaire

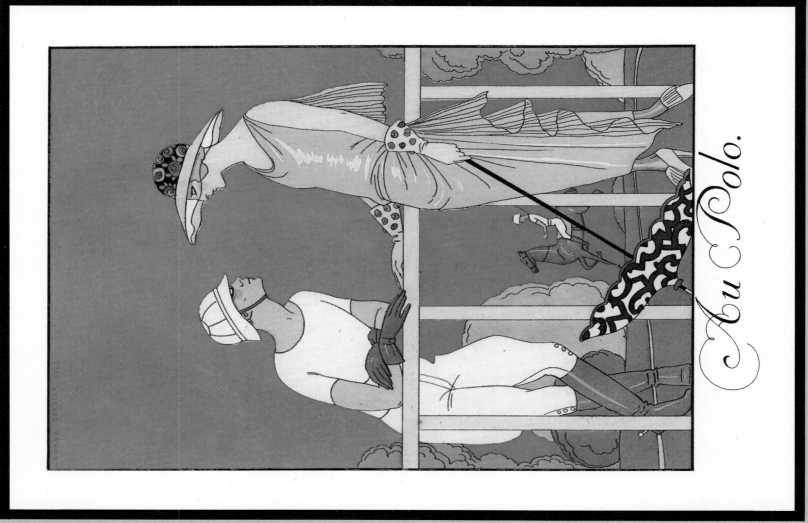

Au Polo.

PLATE 21

Left: Au polo (At polo). *The player
wears an unusual singlet, breeches and boots;
his companion formal summer dress, the
pleats from the shoulders echoing those at the
sides of her asymmetrically draped skirt.
Gracefully understated, the accessories provide decorative contrast. Her shady hat,
with flower trimmed crown, is similar to one
designed by Jane Blanchot in the 1924* Les
Modes. *The gloves have polka dot cuffs and
the curvacious pagoda-type parasol a
dramatic patterned cover.*

France XXe siècle; *s & d George Barbier
1923; 1924 almanac.*

Right: La jolie insulaire (The pretty
islander) *propositioned by an early nineteenth-century seaman in peaked cap, short
jacket and canvas trousers. Her feather
head-dress and skirt were thought to be
characteristic of the Carib Indians, the
original inhabitants of the West Indies.*

Antilles XIXe siècle; *s & d George
Barbier 1923; 1924 almanac.*

Sérénade

PLATE 22

Sérénade, *a picturesque version of Mexican costume which owed much to that of Spain. The lady wears a full-skirted dress with bólero, her head-dress a tall comb and mantilla. She is serenaded by a young man in typical gaucho costume with sombrero, póncho, sash and flaring trousers.*

Mexique XIX siècle; *s & d GB 23; 1924 almanac.*

Comptez sur mes serments.

Sont-ils gentils !

PLATE 23

Left: Sont-ils gentils! (Aren't they sweet!) *A girl from Berne wears the sort of dress considered typically Swiss with wide-brimmed straw hat, blouse with full sleeves and floral bodice. The young man, so elegant in his ribbon-trimmed waistcoat and pleated linen breeches, is difficult to place even from the early nineteenth-century costume books that were Barbier's source for his regional drawings. Despite the caption, there were few pictorial sources for Swiss regional dress before the early nineteenth century.*

Suisse XVIIIᵉ siècle; *s & d George Barbier 1923; 1924 almanac.*

Right: Comptez sur mes serments (I will keep my vows). *A mid-eighteenth-century Hungarian hussar departs for the wars wearing the most glamorous of uniforms, with a feather panache on his cap and a leopard lining to his dolman jacket. His lady wears a rather stagy version of eighteenth-century dress, in real life never so décolleté as it appears here.*

Hongrie XVIIIᵉ siècle; *s & d George Barbier 1923; 1924 almanac.*

La Bénédiction Paternelle

Le Baiser dérobé.

PLATE 24

Left: Le baiser dérobé (The stolen kiss).
*The girl wears the dress typical of Lucerne
with an elaborately trimmed straw hat,
short-sleeved blouse with deep pleated collar
and an embroidered bodice enriched with
chains and a portrait of the Virgin. The
lad is more difficult to place for skull caps,
short-sleeved shirts and pleated linen breeches
were worn in Freiburg and Appenzell. He
has the wide leather belt of the former and
the red jacket of the latter. Traditional
peasant costume differs according to region
and Swiss cantons were very separatist —
details irrelevant to an artist.*

Suisse XVIIIᵉ siècle; *s George Barbier;
1924 almanac.*

Right: La bénédiction paternelle (The
father's blessing). *The old man seems to
have come from Toggenburg where much-
buttoned eighteenth-century-type suits with
deep cuffs were worn through the eighteenth
to the nineteenth century. He blesses a girl
who by her dress is possibly from Thurgovie,
near Lake Constance, and a lad who may
have come from Appenzell. Note the
pleated breeches and footless stockings.*

Suisse XVIIIᵉ siècle; *s & d G. Barbier
1923; 1924 almanac.*

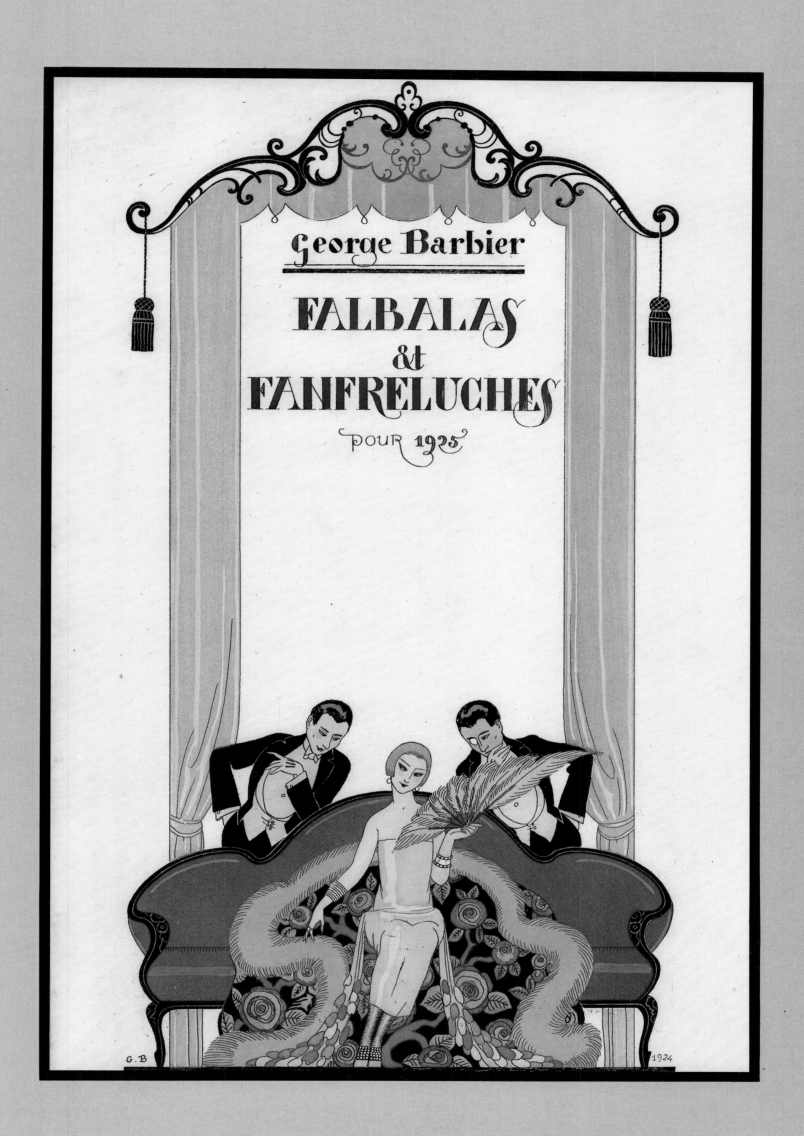

PLATE 25

The cover of the Falbalas et Fanfreluches *almanac of 1925.*

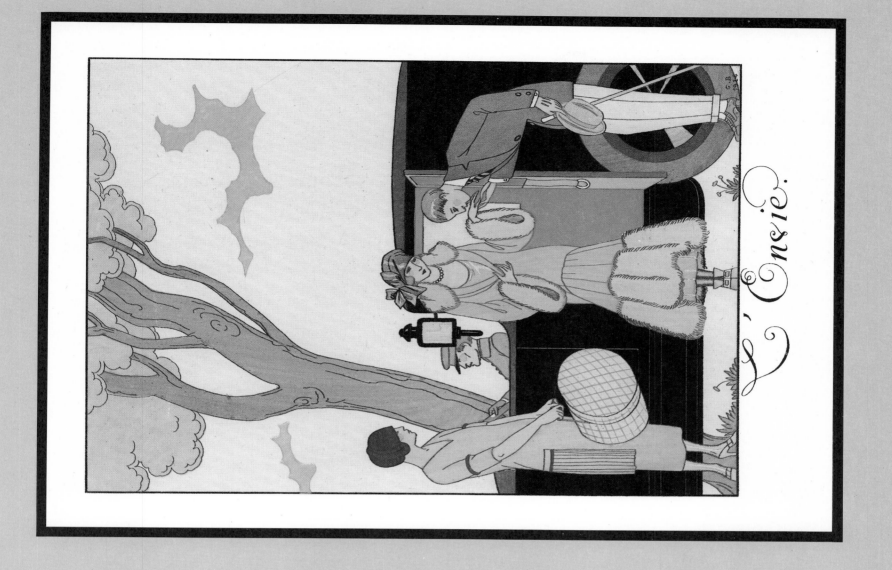

L'Envie.

L'Ivresse

PLATE 26

Left: L'avarice (Meanness). *The lady refusing the pleas of her passionate suitor, already has a great deal: pearls at ears and wrists and a very fashionable evening dress, possibly by Worth from the 1923–24 collection, a décolleté sheath with heavy fur-trimmed hem. Her watchful friend wears one of the modish large-patterned shawls.*

France XXᵉ siècle; *s & d George Barbier 1924; 1925 almanac.*

Right: L'envie (Envy). *The lady stepping from her chauffeur-driven cabriolet limousine wears a coat with flaring fur-trimmed sleeves and hem which she might have purchased from Worth who produced a similar design that year. Her lady's maid wears the simple under-stated dress considered suitable for a personal servant, with modest vee-neck and half-length sleeves, but the pleated panels on the skirt are a fashionable touch. The young man dressed for a summer stroll in town has a long tight jacket and full-cut short grey flannel trousers. He is informal not casual and has hat, gloves, and a light walking cane.*

France XXᵉ siècle; *s & d G.B. 1924; 1925 almanac.*

La Colère.

PLATE 27

La colère (Anger), *displayed by a lady in a tightly fitting two-piece outfit, the hem of the tunic emphasized by a wide band of peasant-style embroidery which matches the cuffs of her gauntlet gloves. Her stubby umbrella, typical for the date, matches her natty red and black shoes. Shoes are also the main dress feature of her sober suited and chastened companion. Is it his flashy high-heeled patent and lizard footwear which was the provocation or the lady speeding away in the background?*

France XXe siècle; *s & d George Barbier 1924; 1925 almanac.*

la Luxure.

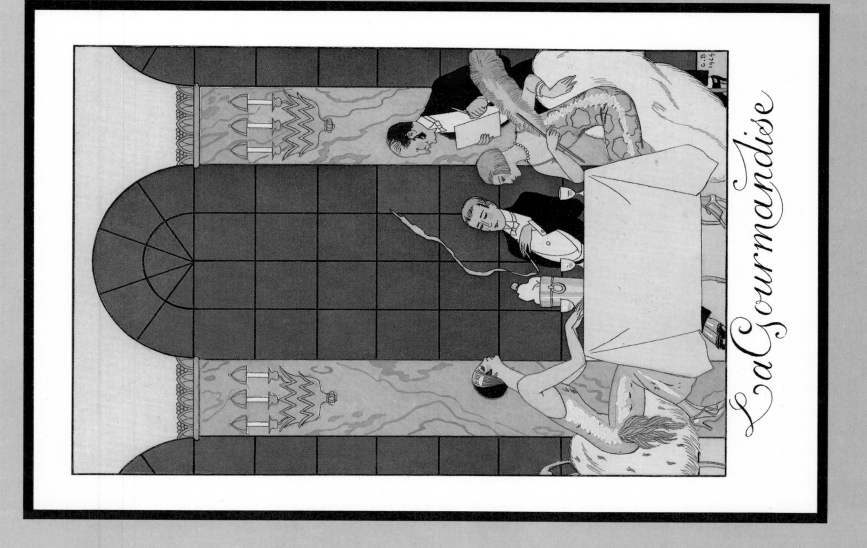

La Gourmandise

PLATE 28

Left: La gourmandise (Gluttony). *The luxury of 1920s café society epitomized by a young man with a pair of lady guests, each ordering a dinner which it seems improbable their tight sheath dresses will allow them to accommodate. The dresses, décolleté, simply cut, depend for effect on all-over beaded patterns, an expensive feature. Note also their luxurious fur wraps. On the whole, the ladies are more ostentatious than fashionable. The single feather plume fan was a typical accessory of the decade.*

France XXᵉ siècle; *s & d G.B. 1924; 1925 almanac.*

Right: La luxure (Pleasure). *A cool pool on a hot day has tempted the ladies to shed their flimsy summer clothes to bathe, undeterred by the proximity of a peeping Tom, an oriental gardener to judge by the hat. An unexpectedly practical touch is the girl trying to loop up her long hair. Wet hair was always a problem for non-shingled lady swimmers in the 1920s.*

France XXᵉ siècle; *s & d G.B. 1924; 1925 almanac.*

La Paresse

L'Orgueil

PLATE 29

Left: L'orgueil (Pride). *During the 1920s Barbier designed many splendid costumes and settings for the* Folies Bergère *and other Paris theatres. Extravagant trappings and trimmings to enhance naked and beautiful bodies were something for which the Paris stage was famous.*

France XXᵉ siècle; *s & d G.B. 1924; 1925 almanac.*

Right: La paresse (Laziness), *displayed by ladies utterly relaxed in Eastern-style pyjamas. Introduced towards the end of the nineteenth century, they became very popular for leisure as well as night wear during the 1920s. Overhead fly fantastic oriental birds of dreams. The scene resembles* Le Pavot (*poppy*) *in the parallel series* Belles du jour. *Hashish and opium smoking were among the society vices in the 1920s.*

France XXᵉ siècle: *s & d G.B. 1924; 1925 almanac.*

La Cruche cassée.

La Souris

PLATE 30

Left: La souris (The mouse) *frightens a lady in a fashionable formal* robe de style, *with low-cut back and full, triple-tiered skirt trimmed with posies. Romantic dresses inspired by mid-Victorian styles were fashionable throughout the 1920s for formal and summer wear. They were the specialities of the couture house of Lanvin.*

France XXᵉ siècle; *s G.B.; 1925 almanac.*

Right: La cruche cassée (The broken jug). *A theatrical version of a gallant eighteenth-century encounter. She wears peasant dress, useful for showing off a pretty figure, and he a rather too short and tight coat and breeches. The jug (the crack almost hidden here) was supposed to symbolize a maiden's virtue.*

France XVIIIᵉ siècle; *s & d G. Barbier; 1925 almanac.*

Colin-Maillard

Pæstum.

PLATE 31

Left: Paestum. *The classical beauty of these Greek temples in southern Italy is the setting for a fashionable little drama. The grieving lady wears a patterned summer two-piece with a three-quarter length tunic, a matching deep-crowned cloche hat, and shoes which tone with her outfit. Equally fashionable is the young man in his tight double-breasted three-piece suit. He wears matching tan accessories, all in very good taste except for his surely excessively high-heeled shoes!*

France XXᵉ siècle; *s & d G.B. 1924; 1925 almanac.*

Right: Colin-maillard (Blind man's buff) *as played perhaps at the court of Louis XVI and Marie Antoinette. The young man wears a simple semi-formal outfit but the ladies are dressed in the fashionable extreme of formal dress with towering head-dresses and much-trimmed gowns supported by side hoops. Barbier knew and loved eighteenth-century costume but photographs of his cinema and theatrical productions suggest that his designs were often amended for a 1920s audience.*

France XVIIIᵉ siècle; *s & d G. Barbier 1924; 1925 almanac.*

"Il était une fois"

PLATE 32

Il était une fois (Once upon a time).
*Breton dress was the most picturesque of
France's many regional costumes, and their
fairy-tales and legends were world famous.
Men's dress was characterized by braid-
trimmed short jackets and pleated linen
trousers. Women's caps differed according
to area. This old lady comes from Finisterre.*

France XIXe siècle; *s G.B.; 1925
almanac.*

PLATE 33

The cover of the Falbalas et Fanfreluches *almanac of 1926.*

L'Air

GEORGE BARBIER 1925

La Terre

GEORGE BARBIER 1925

PLATE 34

Left: La terre (Earth), *and enjoying its fruits is a lady in a sleeveless low-necked shift dress. The cravat front panel was a feature popular in 1926 and appears several times in the fashion magazines. The lady with the spade wears a simple tunic top with colourful binding: the type of garment which made home dressmaking so easy in the 1920s. Her skirt is rather looser and longer than was fashionable, but then Barbier did not really like short skirts. The small boy wears shorts with button shoulder straps and a check shirt, and has his hair arranged in a unisex bob.*

France XXe siècle; *s & d George Barbier 1925; 1926 almanac.*

Right: L'air, *and the autumn breezes have dislodged even the fashionably deep-crowned toques. The lady's dress is conservatively styled, with medium-long full skirt, but an up-to-date full sleeve. Art deco rose-pattern prints were fashionable through the 1920s. Critics, including Barbier, often referred disparagingly to the unisex fashion for cropped hair but though the lady's curls toss gracefully, the man's have merely broken loose from their brilliantine.*

France XXe siècle; *s & d George Barbier 1925; 1926 almanac.*

L'Eau

Le Feu

PLATE 35

Left: Le feu (Fire) *and the fireworks
bursting behind the passionate embrace on
the terrace illuminate a lady in a gown rather
old-fashioned by the mid 1920s, very
décolleté, with a long floating skirt draped
asymmetrically into the low flower-trimmed
waistline. Nevertheless, the soft sentimental
dress contrasts agreeably with her sleek
short hair style. Protecting her finery from
the cold balustrade is a Spanish-style shawl.*

France XXe siècle; *s & d G. Barbier
1925; 1926 almanac.*

Right: L'eau (Water), *and by it, shaded
by typically Japanese artistic accessories of
waving foliage and a parasol, is a bathing
party. The snug fitting bathing costumes
were probably made from silk or wool
jersey and Barbier, like other contemporary
observers, found them saggy, clinging and
unbecoming when wet: a problem he dodges,
for the androgynous figure leaving the water
has nothing on at all. Note the turban-tied
scarf to protect the hair: early bathing caps
were not popular.*

France XXe siècle; *s & d G. Barbier
1925; 1926 almanac.*

L'Été

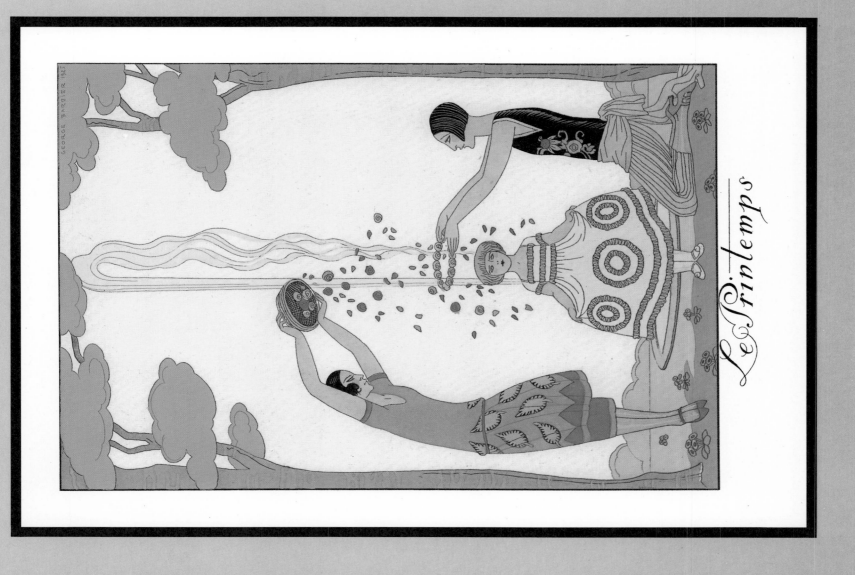

Le Printemps

PLATE 36

Left: Le printemps (Spring), *and showering with flowers the little girl in her Lanvin-style dress are ladies in the shorter sleeker styles of 1925. The girl kneeling displays the new, more angular, cropped hair style.*

France XXe siècle; *s & d George Barbier 1925; 1926 almanac.*

Right: L'été (Summer), *and enjoying it a very fashionable group in evening dress and somewhat classical pose. The standing ladies wear dresses similar to Worth designs, though his crossover hip drapes were sleeker than those of Barbier. The lady in the hammock wears a transparent tunic over her beaded dress, the design of which recalls a model by Doucet illustrated in* Les Modes *for 1924. Armfuls of large African-type bracelets were a fashion feature after the Paris Colonial Exhibition of 1922.*

France XXe siècle; *s & d George Barbier 1925; 1926 almanac.*

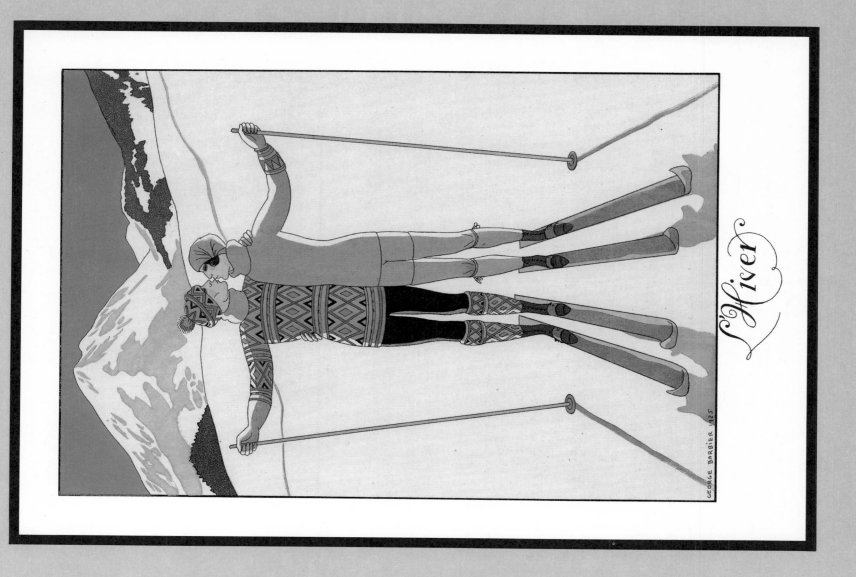

L'Hiver

GEORGE BARBIER 1925

L'Automne

GEORGE BARBIER 1925

PLATE 37

Left: L'automne, *and doves flutter round the couple seated at the feet of Eros the god of love. The Eton-cropped girl is most up to date but in deference to Barbier's preferences still wears her skirts unfashionably low over her knees. Her bolero jacket and wide-brimmed hat suggest Mexican influence, her zigzag-patterned scarf is uncompromisingly modernist. Her companion wears a fashionable informal suit with long fitted jacket and pale contrast trousers. In England and the United States suits were beginning to become looser and more square cut by the mid 1920s; not so in France.*

France XXᵉ siècle; *s & d George Barbier 1925; 1926 almanac.*

Right: L'hiver (Winter), *and the look-alike androgynous couple are posed with stark modernist symmetry below the snowy Japanese-style mountains. By the 1920s winter sports had become very popular, and the clothes featured in the fashion magazines are utilitarian and unisex. Knitwear was a significant fashion feature at the time.*

France XXᵉ siècle; *s & d George Barbier 1925; 1926 almanac.*

Le Soir

Le Matin

PLATE 38

Left: Le matin (Morning). *An eighteenth-century-type Venus rises from her
rococo cockle shell bed, her very non-
eighteenth-century skimpy nightwear ap-
parently as shocking to the portrait of her
noble protector, whose likeness hangs overhead, as to the peeping Tom behind the
curtains. Barbier was fond of the works of
Boucher and Fragonard, painters of several
similar slightly risqué scenes, as well as
intrigued by the many gallant adventures of
Casanova.*

France XVIII siècle; *s & d George
Barbier 1925; 1926 almanac.*

Right: Le soir (Evening). *In a characteristic combination of 1920s cosmopolitan
aesthetic influences, the lady in her exotic
beaded Parisian sheath dress stands im-
pervious and indifferent in front of a lacquer
screen depicting a glacial Japanese mountain
landscape.* The French Colonial *exhibition
took place in 1922, and she wears African-
type bangles from elbow to wrist and carries
a fan in the same style. The little pagan god
on the pedestal is as unmoved by the young
man's passion as is the lady.*

France XXe siècle; *s & d G. Barbier
1925; 1926 almanac.*

Les Cerises

PLATE 39

Les cerises (Cherries). *Eighteenth-century ladies' underwear generally did not include drawers, a characteristic exploited by many painters of* scènes gallantes, *such as Boucher, Fragonard and Watteau. The pretty lady in her too short and very theatrical eighteenth-century-style outfit must have been tempting the young man with more than fresh fruit. There are echoes of Rousseau, the philosopher's cherry-picking exploits with Mlle Galley, mentioned in his* Confessions, *in 1731.*

France XVIIIᵉ siècle; *s & d GB 1925; 1926 almanac.*

Le Modèle Intéressant

PLATE 40

Le modèle intéressant (The interesting model). *A mid-nineteenth-century painter much less elegant than Barbier was said to have been, commemorates the 1920s version of a Victorian lady with a small boy. The child wears an updated, rather scanty Highland costume of the type that French ladies had been imposing on their offspring ever since the style was first introduced by Queen Victoria for her children in the 1840s.*

France XIXe siècle; *s & d G. Barbier 25; 1926 almanac.*